Yours Truly,

Kalliope

Yours Truly, Kalliope

KALLIOPE KAY

Illustrated by Keller Makemson

THE OUTSIDER **POET PRESS**

Baltimore, Maryland

The Outsider Poet Press
@outsiderpoetpress
outsiderpoetpress.com

ISBN: 13-978-1-959373-09-4

Cover and Book Design by Keller Makemson
@kmakemson.design
kmakemson.com

For anyone who has ever felt
just a little lost and alone,

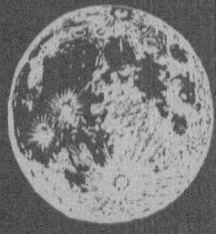

never forget that
life ebbs and flows.

Preface

Dear Reader,

Your late teens and early twenties are hard. You leave your childhood behind and enter a new world full of responsibility. *Life ebbs and flows.* It is unpredictable and demanding, all whilst you navigate major life changes and decisions. It's difficult and it's lonely. Your peers are all at different stages of their lives. Some of your friends are getting married and having children, while others still live at home. Somewhere along the way, you find yourself—but you also lose a lot of yourself in the process.

My teenage years and early twenties were no different, except there was a global pandemic that further complicated things (hello class of 2020), and ultimately ended my long-distance relationship with the man I thought I was going to marry. I was shouldering a lot of childhood trauma and mental health problems that I had suppressed and bottled up instead of addressing. I was carrying around a lot of hurt, and the negativity was shaping me into a person I didn't want to be. I needed an outlet for all of my pain, *so I started writing.*

Yours Truly, Kalliope started out as a note in my phone titled "The Rants and Rambles of a Twenty-Something," and that's exactly what they were. *Rants and Rambles*. Over the past three years, these rants and rambles evolved into poems compiled in a google document—a diary of sorts. These poems were deeply personal. They detailed my darkest secrets, my biggest insecurities, and all of my struggles—but also my greatest triumphs. I finally found the words that I didn't have the strength to speak, and I had no intention of sharing them with anyone.

But my dear friend Lyra Wren (@poetrybylyra) convinced me otherwise. I started posting my work on TikTok using a pen name. Anonymity granted me the freedom to be authentic and vulnerable, without the fear of judgment or backlash. It empowered me to talk about my trauma and open up about my struggles instead of hiding what I was going through. It was incredibly gratifying to see how other people resonated with my work. I found a community in the other writers on TikTok and my following. Ten thousand followers later, Outsider Poet Press signed a publishing contract with me.

This book is a collection of poems that deal with some pretty heavy themes, but ultimately *Yours Truly, Kalliope* documents my ongoing healing journey through poetry. The book is split into four different sections: *The Breaking*, *The Baring*, *The Becoming*, and *The Blossoming*.

It's scary to be vulnerable, to open yourself up unapologetically, and I am terrified to expose this part of myself to the world, but I am also so excited. This is my story. This is me in my entirety—*the good, the bad, and the ugly*. I hope that others read my poems and feel seen. Whatever you are going through, *know that you are not alone*.

Yours Truly,

Kalliope

Contents

Content Warning

The following content contains references to:

- anxiety
- body dysmorphia
- disordered eating
- depression
- explicit language
- infidelity
- religious trauma
- sexual content
- suicidal ideation
- as well as other tough topics.

Please read what you need and leave the rest.

My depression and anxiety
whittled away at me
until I was a husk
of the girl I used to be.

So I *sharpened* my anger,
my heartbreak, my tears,
my bitterness, my despair,
my loneliness, my rage,

and *honed* it all into a blade that
I used to carve my pain into prose

and called it poetry.

The Breaking

(Present Participle)

[brākiNG]

separate or cause to separate into pieces as a
result of a blow, shock, or strain.

Before this life took its toll,
she was *just a little girl*

with two pigtail braids
and freckled cheeks,
a gap-toothed smile
and sunflowers for eyes.

That little girl chased fireflies
until the stars twinkled in the sky,
and her nightlight would keep
the worst of her monsters at bay.

But sometime between then and today,
this world swallowed her whole

and spit out a *weary woman*.

 - *swallowed whole*

If you looked at her
you'd never know
how *irrevocably broken*
she really was.

Because she bottled
all of her pain up inside
and refused to
let them see her cry.

She carried her exhaustion
in the bruises beneath her eyes,
and her spine bent beneath
the weight of her depression.
She ate her emotions while
anxiety ate away at her body.

But people do not notice
the wounds they cannot see,
so she suffered in silence

and spent her youth
bleeding internally.

     - internal bleeding

My heart aches for the little girl
with sunflowers for eyes.

The naive child who
constantly overwatered plants
simply because she didn't know
how to *stop giving*.

And she never learned.

She grew up to be a woman
who fills others' glasses,
even when there is
nothing left in hers.

    - *drained*

It's just how we show our love, they say.

It begins as light-hearted jabs,
but then the teasing evolves
into something *more* in the end.

But they do not see how deep
their words have cut me.
They cannot see the scars
they left on my psyche.

Sure, they made me tough,
they gave me thick skin—

but I was just a kid.

     - thick skin

I mourn the child
I never got to be,
because the order of my birth
shaped my *entire identity*.

It is the curse of the eldest daughter
to bear the weight of the world
on shoulders that are far too frail
with *no one* to lighten her load.

I am how I am because I had to be.
Burdened with responsibility
and eager to please,
I became what they demanded.

Mature for my age,
they said I had an *old soul*,
reliable and steady.
I became independent

and I grinned and bore it.

    - grin and bear it

You called me *selfish*.

You characterized me
as an *ungrateful bitch*,
and labeled me a
lazy piece of shit.

But you didn't know
that I was just trying
to keep myself alive.

I was just trying to make it
through another night.

I was just trying to survive.

    - survival mode

"And I can go anywhere I want, just not home."

I must have listened to that
Taylor Swift lyric a thousand times
but it still didn't quite prepare me
for when that reality became mine.

Ensnared by the trappings that come with age,
my parents sold my childhood home,
then packed my girlhood into cardboard boxes
and moved twenty-two hours away.

My best friends now live in different states
and my circle grows smaller with each passing year.
There is no one to blame for this pain—
I grew up, I got older—but I *can't* go back.

I *have* to move on.

Now eternally damned
to watch my grandparents get older
and my little brother grow up through
photographs and facetime calls.

Stuck observing my best friends' lives
through social media posts on my phone,
fated to be forever just a visitor in my parent's home,
as the ache of adulthood settles into my bones.

    - *growing pains*

My *own mother* told me that
I'd make a terrible mom.
She was just kidding—
at least, I *think* she meant it in jest.

But that one tore a hole
right through my chest.

In that moment, I knew
that *nothing* I ever do
would be *good enough* for her.

So I bit my tongue until it bled
and hid away my rage,
the pain diminishing with
distance and age.

But no matter how far I run,
I cannot escape
the voice in my head,
nor the blood in my veins.

I cannot escape my *DNA*.

- *blood ties*

I remember being mesmerized
as my Art History professor
flipped through slides of
women painted in the Renaissance.

These women are *art*,
and I see *my body*
reflected in their imagery.

Their names are lost to history
but their fuller figures
are enshrined in gilded frames
for all of posterity.

Immortalized by the masters of old,
they are venerated for
their curves and porcelain skin.
They are *celebrated* for the
very things that I am *ridiculed*.

Born a *quincentenary* too late,
my worth is reduced to the numbers on the scale,
my value correlates to the size of my jeans,
when I drop a number, my merit increases.

I can't help but think
if only I had been born in the Renaissance.

- *renaissance woman*

I am my own worst enemy—
I *constantly* ridicule my body,
analyzing every bump and mark,
every *so-called abnormality* that I see:

the rolls of fat on my belly
the cellulite on my thighs
the stretchmarks on my hips
the birthmark on my shoulder
the scar on my shin
the callus on my finger
the strands of hair on my chin

I label them all as *flaws*,
because that's what society taught me.

   - flaws

As the days grow shorter
and the cold seeps in,
4 am has become
my *dearest friend.*

Night after night
I lay awake
all alone in my bed,
pleading with my ceiling.

Watching the fan spin around
like the thoughts in my head,
so I confide in the moon
until dusk fades into dawn

and weariness settles
into my bones.

- *insomniac*

I long for those lunchbox days
where my *nightlight*
could scare the worst
of my monsters away.

- *nightlights*

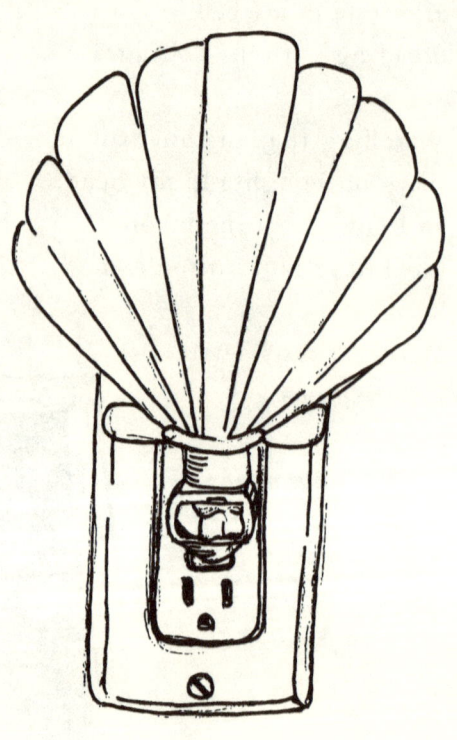

I confide in the man
in the moon each night
but he *never* replies,

so I converse with Venus
about my loneliness
and divulge my anger
and rage to Mars.

I wish on every shooting star,
telling them of all
my hopes and dreams,
while I disclose my fears
and anxieties to Mercury.

But more often than not,
I hear no response,
so I close my eyes
and count sheep

yet sleep always evades me.

    - counting sheep

"*OhMyGoSh do they have an accent?*"
is always the first thing out of their mouths,
and that fall semester of freshman year
is all butterflies and sparks.

Then Thanksgiving break comes around,
but it's only *a few days*,
and then there's winter break,
but it's only a *month* apart.

Three months in summer,
that will be the worse you think—
but then there's a global pandemic
and three months turn into *over a year*
of not knowing when you'll see them again.

People tell you *long distance* is hard,
but that doesn't even begin to cover it.
A *seven-hour* time difference,
some days you wake up
to their good night texts,

and there are nights that
you cry yourself to sleep
all alone in your bed,
stifling your sobs in your pillow
so as not to wake up
your little brother next door.

You'd give anything
to reach through that phone,
for them to wrap you in their arms,
for their lips to kiss your tears away,
to even just hear their voice
not distorted by FaceTime.

There are days that it feels
like an utter impossibility,
but you cling onto the hope
that this separation is *just temporary.*

But the worst part is
after enduring all of that
for *four fucking years,*
we still didn't make it.

     - *long distance love*

I remember our last night
like it was only yesterday.

I sobbed into your chest
as you held me tight
and kissed all of
my tears away.

You tried to assuage my fears
by whispering reassurances in my ear
that it would be alright,
and that *we would be okay.*

You told me the distance had nothing on us,
that the miles would not tear us apart,
because what we had was forever,
and I had your whole heart.

You said that this separation was only temporary,
that we would be reunited once again
because I would be your wife someday,
and *it would all be worth it in the end.*

But deep down I think I already knew,
that *this was the last time I'd hold you.*

- *our last night*

I visited my college town for the first time
since graduation, and when I looked
around my old stomping grounds,
all I could see was the ghost of *you and me.*

I knew the painting building was *haunted,*
but old memories of us
lingered in every single corner
of the whole damn campus.

The freshman dorm where we first kissed
The cobblestone stairs where you always held my hand
The bleachers where I watched you play
The locker room where you'd meet me after my games
The ceramics building where you'd walk me home
The courtyard where I first said I loved you
The fast-food restaurant we had our biggest fight
The dive bar where we stay up late Thursday nights

And finally, the parking lot where we parted
with teary-eyed kisses and a "see you soon,"
not knowing that it would be the last time,
not knowing that it was goodbye.

And on the car ride home, *I cried.*

- *ghost town*

They tell me that
April showers bring May flowers,
that there is a reason
for all this rain—

but all that May brought me
was an abundance of
heartache and misery,
sadness and pain.

    - may's misery

One day I will tell my kids about you,
how we met and fell in love.
But saying *"my kids"* tastes
bitter on my tongue,

because it will not be the story
of how I met their father.

They will not be *our children.*

Three kids, we always said
but family tradition dictates
that the oldest must
inherit my middle name.

And I don't even know if *I want kids* anymore.
I jokingly say that I'm just going to own dogs,

but I'm only *half-kidding.*

If I do happen to become a mother someday,
the eldest will still have my middle name.
but the last name on their birth certificate
will always look just a little *off.*

    - *baby names*

You knew all of my best stories—
you helped me write some after all.
You laughed at the terrible jokes
I learned from my father.

We talked about our dreams
about the future we'd build together.
We picked out our children's names
and talked about engagement rings.

"I'd only say yes if it came with a puppy,"
I teased, but *you knew better.*

And I'd have said yes in a heartbeat,
because you were my happily ever after,

but *she* was your forever.

    - engagement rings

You looked me in the eyes
and *promised me forever*,
which we sealed with a kiss
and a pinky swear.

But now I see that
it was all just pretty lies,
and I was only nineteen
when my girlhood died.

You took advantage
of my naivety
and coerced your way
between my sheets.

I thought I gave myself to you freely,
but you stole my innocence

and then betrayed me.

  - betrayal

My mind was reeling
I couldn't believe what I was seeing.

I went over to your place that night
fully intending to end it, to end us,
because I said from the beginning
that *I don't date cheaters.*

But that night there were tears
streaming down both of our cheeks
and you got down on your knees
swearing it was *just that one time.*

You promised that
we could get past this,
that we would be fine,
because you were *mine.*

In that moment I knew
I wasn't ready to lose you,
to jeopardize *three years* together
for just *one drunken night.*

I rationalized *was it really cheating*
if you were drinking?

So I let the arms that betrayed me
hold me while the hands
that had gripped her hips
wiped my tears away.

But the damage was done
and that was the *beginning of our end*.

    - *D.O.D.*

They say that
it only takes
sixty-six days
to form a new habit.

Well, my love, we had
one thousand
three hundred
and six days
to build ours.

So please tell me why
it took you less than
fourteen days to
throw it all away?

And why I still cannot stop sleeping
on the left side of the bed?

     - *habits*

Fuck you.

Fuck you for saying that you loved me,
for making me think that you cared.
Fuck you for promising me forever
and sealing it with a kiss and a pinky swear.

Fuck you for coercing your way between
my knees and my sheets
when I was only nineteen.
Fuck you for being the cause of
the tears running down my cheeks.

Fuck you for betraying me, then
pledging me fidelity from your knees.
Fuck you for erasing me and then replacing me
within the span of *two fucking weeks.*

But most of all,

Fuck you for making me
question *the whole damn thing.*

      - fuck you

"I'm sorry," slips off my tongue
as easily as the air from my lungs.
I feel an overwhelming need
to constantly apologize

even if I did nothing wrong.

    - apologies

She pasted a smile on her face
that never quite reached her eyes,
and hid behind the words *"I'm fine."*

She said it so often
that she *almost* had herself
convinced of her own lies.

    - masking

I read somewhere that the body's
stress response to *anxiety*
is to shunt one's blood
away from one's extremities.

No wonder I am always cold,
and my fingers are constantly blue.

Anxiety has already *robbed* me
of my inner peace—
apparently it is now *stealing*
all of my warmth, too.

    - stress response

I call my old friends
but all they ever ask me
is if I have met someone,
and am finally dating again.

So I stopped calling first

I watched my circle dwindle,
getting *smaller and smaller*,
as the birthday texts got
fewer with each passing year.

I chalked it up to getting older
and moving to a different state.

I told myself that I was *busy*,
protecting my peace
and *focusing on me*,
but I was really just *self-isolating*,

and *nobody* noticed as I faded away.

    - forgotten

To all the friends I've lost,
it's your birthday today.

I erased it from my calendar,
but I never could delete it from my brain.

I know *we don't speak any more,*
but I still have your number saved,
so I picked up my phone
and almost called you anyway.

But each time I hovered over your name,
I couldn't help but hesitate.

So instead, I typed out a text
that I will never send,
only to delete it and retype it,
then delete it all over again.

    - birthday texts

I try to tell myself that *it's fine*
that I skipped breakfast this morning
because *it's just gonna be this one time,*
but in my heart I know that's a lie.

I can feel myself slipping into old habits
as "Do you want to grab dinner?"
becomes "I already ate"
or "I'm not hungry."

I can feel the ache of hunger
gnawing away at my belly
as I lose my energy
and begin to waste away.

I know that *it's not healthy,*
but I keep doing it anyway.

Even though I know *it's not good for me*
that doesn't stop me from binging,
and then replacing my avocado toast
with *just a cup of coffee.*

  - *relapsing*

I have been to rock bottom.

It's a pretty dismal place
with not a single friendly face.

In rock bottom,
the world stops spinning,
the sun doesn't shine,
and the birds don't sing.

It looks different to everybody,
but for me rock bottom looked
like sitting in my bathtub
under a stream of scalding water
with no more tears to shed,
just wanting to be dead.

But I picked myself up
off that shower floor.
I crawled my way
out of rock bottom.

And I will never go back there again.

    - rock bottom

The Baring

(Present Participle)

[beriNG]

uncovering (a part of the body or other thing)
and exposing it to view.

They love me,
they love me not.

She plucked her petals *one by one*,
baring it all and giving
them *everything* she had
until she was left with *none*.

    - bare

We poets romanticize mental illness,
we call our brokenness beautiful
and try to find a lesson in
our anxiety and depression.

But sometimes *rain is just rain*,
and there are no flowers
that sprout from our pain.

Sometimes there is no
dancing in mud puddles
or searching for rainbows.

Sometimes it's just
weathering the storm.
without logical reason or
rational explanation.

Sometimes there is
no bright side,
no person to blame,
nothing to save.

Because sometimes
it's just *ugly*.

     - *ugly truths*

Growing up, I always
just wanted to be *enough*.

But I took on *too much*:
4.5 GPA, Honor Roll, AP Classes,
after-school clubs and extracurriculars,
a three-sport student-athlete, working part-time
so I never had to ask my parents for a dime,
academic, art, and athletic scholarships,
working three jobs,
incapable of saying no.
It didn't matter.
It—I—was *never enough*.

Now I am trying to slow down,
to unlearn these tendencies

and just be *enough for me*.

- pathological people pleaser

I do not understand how
we had the same childhood,
but both of my brothers
walked away *unscathed*,

while I drag my baggage
beside me every single day.

I can't help but feel guilty,
because I grew up with
two parents who loved me,
but I am still *struggling*.

I think that there might be
something wrong with me.

    - black sheep

When I was six,
I was told I was *too bossy.*

When I was ten,
I was told that I was *too loud.*

When I was twelve,
I was told that I talked *too much.*

When I was fourteen,
I was told that I was *too opinionated.*

When I was sixteen,
I was told that I was *too outspoken.*

When I was eighteen,
I was told that I was *too impulsive.*

When I was twenty-one,
I was told that I was *too selfish.*

Now I am twenty-four years old,
but when I visit my parent's house
I still switch my nose ring for a stud.
I wear long sleeves to hide my tattoos.
And I don't pack ripped jeans.

I filter who I am
and suppress my trauma
to make myself more palatable,
to avoid judgment and drama.

I am left torn between
being *unapologetically me*,
respecting tradition,
and appeasing my family.

    - filtered

They say that your early twenties are *lonely*,

but there has not been a single day
that I have not carried my exhaustion
in the bags beneath my eyes,
too tired to cry myself to sleep most nights.

There has not been a single week
that anxiety did not cling onto me,
or that depression did not
make a home in my bones.

So I guess I'm *never truly alone.*

　　- constant companions

I cry in the shower
so that *no one sees*
the tears that stream
down my cheeks.

- *shower thoughts*

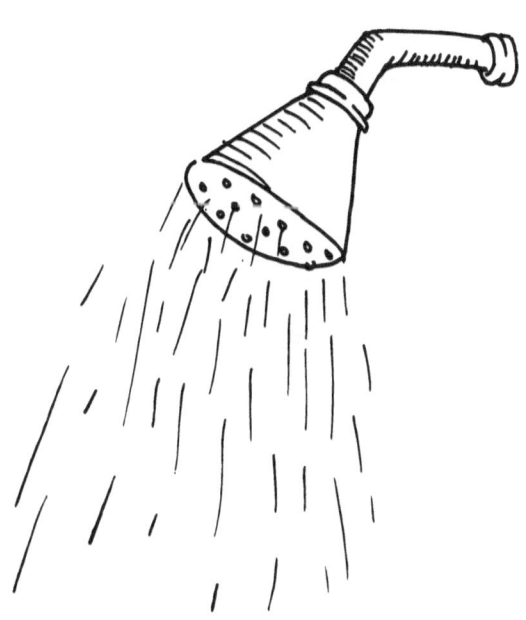

Nostalgia is a fickle thing.

It smells like your cologne
and tastes like my mother's mac 'n' cheese.
It imbues me with warmth
and tinges *reminiscences*
in hues of melancholy.

It is *recollections* of childhood
and a lifetime of *yesterdays*
that bring a smile to my face
and simultaneously fill me with grief.

Nostalgia brings me to my knees
and causes me to weep
as *memories* leak out my eyes
and roll down my cheeks.

     - *nostalgia*

Oh God, please hear me
used to be my nightly plea.
I would pray on my knees
begging for just one sign.

But somewhere along the way
my faith went to an early grave—
I lost my religion
and buried my beliefs.

But I am still haunted by what
these *Good Christians* teach.

Love thy neighbor as thyself,
but that love is conditional.
Accept forgiveness, and forgive others in return,
but anyone who doesn't conform
is *going to hell.*

If they are your shepherds,
I do not wish to be
a part of your flock,
so I will become something they hate

and if I am *damned,*
then let that be my fate.

- shepherds and sheep

Untag, archive, delete.
You purged my presence
from your social media
the same day we parted ways.

Four years' worth of memories
were wiped clean in a blink—
and then you erased me,
then replaced me

within the span of *two weeks.*

    - erased

I used to love telling the story of how we met,
shared glances across a crowded room,
just a boy in a red t-shirt
and a girl in a baseball cap.

It was the story I thought
they'd recount at our wedding,
the tale that I'd tell
our children before bedtime.

But now you're *just another stranger*,
someone that I used to know,
a mutual on my social media
who in the end

I can't even call a *friend*.

And as fucked up as it is,
knowing how it all ends
and everything you did,
I think *I still might do it all again.*

     - our story

I saw photos of *you and her*
on your mum's Facebook feed,
smiling and dancing and eating cake
at your grandparents' 75th anniversary.

She was wearing my favorite color,
and everyone looked so happy—
I bet they fell in love with her
almost as quickly as you got over me.

And I know that ultimately
our situation was tricky,
that *no* long-distance relationship
is ever particularly easy.

That ours was complicated by
the ocean separating you and me,
not to mention a global pandemic
and our different nationalities.

And that in the end
there's no one to blame

not you
not her
not them
not me.

But I can't help but
be filled with envy
that she was the girl
that got to meet your family.

    - envy

I attended a wedding last April
of *two college friends*
who had started dating
the week before us.

After years of waiting,
they finally got to start
their forever, *together*,
and I couldn't have been happier.

But my joy was tainted
all throughout the evening
with a hint of jealousy
and persistent thoughts of

that should've been you and me.

And I cried when
they had their first dance,
but I'm still not sure
who my tears were for:

them or us.

　　　- jaded

"He's a good first boyfriend,"
they always used to say,

and that would drive me *crazy.*

At first, I defended him
until I was blue in the face,
adamant that I was going
to marry that boy someday.

But eventually they
wore me down,
and my protests
died in my throat,

because it was just easier
to bite my tongue until it bled,
to roll my eyes and
retort inside my head.

It kills me to admit it,
but *maybe they were right.*

- good first boyfriend

I thought that you taught me
what love was *supposed to be.*
But in hindsight I see
that all that you taught me

was what love *shouldn't be.*

   - first love

When I turned twenty-two
you were an ocean away,
so I FaceTimed you and cried.

We broke up that following May.

It only took you two weeks
to find her, to fuck her,
and you were dating again
by summertime.

You posted on her twenty-fifth birthday
with a carefully crafted caption
where you used words like
wonderful, proud, and *my beautiful woman.*

While I was a *silly girl*
who had to beg to be posted,
and even then, I was
just *your idiot.*

When I turned twenty-three
you did not text me—
that year, my birthday gift
was *independence and bitterness.*

  - *birthday gift*

With you, I was happy
to do the mundane:

to fold laundry
to make grocery lists
to wash dishes
to talk baby names
and nursery themes

and I would've done it
with a smile on my face
every single day
for the rest of my life.

But you never did intend
to make me *your wife*.

— *playing house*

GROCERY LIST:
eggs
Milk
Bread
Avocados
Strawberries
coffee

I opened myself up to you.

I let you in between my sheets and my knees,
while I shared with you all of
my deepest fears and insecurities,
and included you in my hopes and dreams.

But in my naivety,
I mistook *salt for sugar,*
unable to tell the difference
between briny and sweet,

because for you, *it was never that deep.*

You left me with a festering wound
and a bitter aftertaste on my tongue,
but now I know that there's a difference
between *attention* and *love.*

    - salt in the wound

Four years went by
And I could count
the number of times
you tried your hand
at showing me affection.

I didn't ask for much,
grocery store flowers here and there.
The bar wasn't high,
but you could never meet it,
much less exceed it.

So now I go alone to the
Farmers' Market each week
where the florist knows me by name,
and buy myself a fresh bouquet.

Rationally, I know that
these flowers are only temporary,
they will just wilt and die,
But apparently, darling,

so were you and I.

    - temporary thing

I often write about how *you* killed that girl,
the one with sunflowers for eyes,
how *you* stabbed her in the heart
and made her cry.

But one might argue that the fatal blow
was dealt by *my* hand, not *yours*.
That her death was on *me*—
that it was nothing but *self-inflicted* misery.

Because it was *I* who twisted
that knife between her ribs
and plunged it even deeper
into her chest.

And in the end,
I was just as guilty as *you*.

    - guilty

I can still envision us making dinner
in the kitchen that we painted sage green.
with sleepy eyes and bare feet
and two forgotten glasses of wine.

You are holding me from behind
as I spill something on your favorite t-shirt,
and I giggle as you tell me there's flour in my hair,
but we both know that it's not really there.

It's all forehead kisses
and slow dancing in the light
of the refrigerator late at night,
but we both know that I can't dance.

In my heart I know that it's not real,
because we both know that I can't cook.

> *- kitchen cabinets*

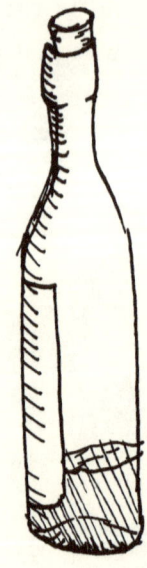

KALLIOPE KAY

If I had known that Sunday morning in March
was the last time I'd see your face,
I think *I would have*
lingered in your embrace.

I would have traced the
scar above your brow
and kissed the dimple
resting on your cheek.

I would have memorized
the shade of your eyes,
the scent of your cologne,
and the taste of your lips.

I would have said goodbye
and allowed myself to cry,

instead of rushing
through our farewell,
attempting to hide the tears
welling in my eyes.

    - farewell

People choose to walk out
of your life one day.

And even though they have
given you no reason to,
you still leave the porch light
on for them each night,

because a small part of you
hopes that they might
once again find themselves
at your *doorstep*.

    - welcome mat

I have a tendency to love deeply
and wear my heart on my sleeve,
to spread myself thin for everybody else
and forget to save some love for *myself*.

    - water colors

I am a Sunday night dinner
with your parents kind of girl,
so why did you make me *hide*
whenever they FaceTimed?

    - *dirty little secret*

It's been *three years*
since I've kissed your lips,
two of those since we called it quits,
and I have not been with anyone since.

I've filled the past few years
with platonic intimacy
and "focusing on me,"
while staying busy.

But the reality is
that I am scared
to open my heart
to another man.

I am scared to get hurt again.

    - confessions

I am absolutely terrified that
I will spend the rest of my life
stuck on the outside.

I fear that I will never be a priority
to the ones who mean the most to me,
because they all have somebody else
while I just have them and myself.

I am scared that I will
forever be the spectator,
watching the camaraderie
from the back seat.

Fated to always be the friend
walking a few steps behind
when there isn't room
next to them on the path,

because when *two* is company
and *three* is a crowd,

I can do the math.

    - third wheel

They say that *hurt people hurt people.*

So I used that as
an excuse to stay single
because I was still hurting
from everything you did to me.

But the reality is that
even though I tried not to,
I still hurt somebody—
I hurt me.

    - hurt

I wish that when I was drowning,
someone had pulled me out of the water,
rather than make it *just another lesson*
and attempt to teach me how to swim.

I wish that when I fell down,
someone had picked me up,
wiped the tears streaming down my cheeks,
and placed Band-Aids on my scraped knees.

I wish I had been hugged more as a kid,
and that "I'm proud of you"
wasn't such a rare occurrence
out of my parents' lips.

I wish I could take my younger self
and wrap her tight in my arms.
I'd tell her that she'll be just fine,
that it's all going to be alright.

But it's so much easier to say all that,
when you're ahead, looking behind—
because *these are the lessons*
that you learn with time.

    - swim lessons

KALLIOPE KAY

You always swore that you'd
buy me an engagement ring
when you had a bit more money,
but honey, here's the thing—

I would have married you
without a cent to your name.

So I spent four years begging for more,
staying when I should have walked away,
because I was good at pretending
that we were going to be okay.

But I was naive to believe
that you would ever change,
and somewhere between
the mediocrity and infidelity

You lost me.

    - losing me

I wish I could say that
I loved myself enough
back then to walk away,
but instead *I stayed.*

And I have carried that guilt
with me every single day,
questioning why I didn't have
the self-respect to end us right then,

because I sure as hell deserved better,
and I will not make the same mistake twice.

  - self-respect

It took me almost twenty-five years
and some therapy to learn
that loving my family
and recognizing how they hurt me

are not mutually exclusive.

That it's okay to talk about
what you've been through
and it does not make you
weak or selfish.

That it does not make you a disappointment
or mean you failed as a daughter.

It does not mean you love them any less.

        - mutually exclusive

My darling child,
you might not see it now,
but there is a blessing
in the breaking.

One day, you will *fill your darkness*
with a whole spectrum of color—
you will take all of your broken pieces
and *create your own rainbows.*

    - *blessing in the breaking*

The Becoming

(Noun)

[bəˈkəmiNG]

the process of coming to be something or
of passing into a state.

My twenties have been a battlefield
on which *I have died a thousand deaths*,
a graveyard littered with casualties
of my broken heart and lost dreams.

I have had to bury so many versions of me,
that I am still haunted by—
visions of who I could have been
and ghosts of the girl I used to be.

Nonetheless, each year on my birthday
I wipe away my tears
and blow out the candles
to celebrate the simple victory

that I am still here,
that I made it to another year.

      - battlefields and birthday candles

She carried her pain in
the bags beneath her eyes
and refused to let
anyone see her cry.

She bottled up all of
her tears and fears
until she was drowning
from the inside.

But she is tired of *pretending*,
and done *hiding* her hurt.

Let it brand her for all to see,
revealing every single flaw
and *exposing* each
of her vulnerabilities.

She doesn't want their pity,
only to be seen in her *entirety*.

      - the good, the bad, and the ugly

I used to believe that *biting my tongue*
was the only way to preserve the peace
and please the people who loved me,
but holding onto that belief cost me dearly.

And the price of suffering in silence was steep.
I sacrificed more than just some sleep
and my mental well-being—
I gave up my authenticity.

But *using my voice*
has brought me the closest
I've felt to inner peace
since I was sixteen.

So I will continue to write poetry,
until I have nothing left to say.

    - why I write

KALLIOPE KAY

I loaded my life into my Civic
and packed my trunk to the brim.
With a full tank and the address
of my new chapter plugged into the GPS,

I was ready to hit the road.

My parents and I said our goodbyes,
I buckled my seatbelt and put my car in drive.
I was determined to not look back,
intent for my eyes to remain dry.

But as I watched them disappear
in my rearview mirror,
my vision began to blur,

and I cried all the way across the state line.

    - long-distance daughter

You are *a whole world* away,

but I find comfort in knowing
that we are looking up
at the *same moon and stars,*
even if *she's* the one in your arms.

      - *same moon and stars*

Unimaginable.
That is my future without you.

I cannot envision a reality
that does not have you in it—
but no matter how hard you try,
you cannot stop time.

Childhood friends lose touch,
and grandparents get older,
while little brothers grow up,
and younger cousins outgrow you.

Your mother gets wrinkles
and your father's beard turns gray.
You move a thousand miles away
and now live in different states.

And yet you are *only a phone call away,*
so I'll dial your number and say your name,

because all we have is *today.*

    - *unimaginable*

He was that girl's *everything*,
and she gave him just that.
Every single molecule in her body
was in love with that boy.

His fingers knew *every* inch of her skin,
and her heart beat for him, *and only him*.
He was the blood running through her veins
and the very air in her lungs.

She would have given him
her kidney if he had asked,
because she swore that
she'd die without him.

But here she is, still breathing—
because I am not that girl *anymore*.

      - lessons from Meredith Grey

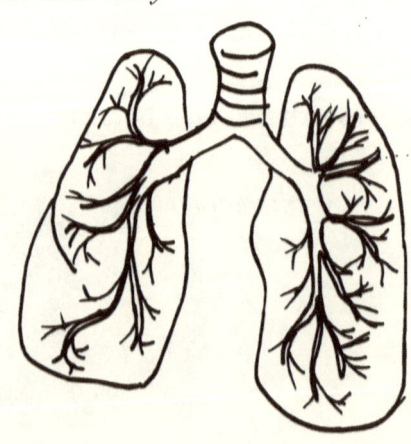

I had dreamt of our future,
of what our life would be,
if not for the ocean
between you and me.

And the funny thing is that
I would've married you in a heartbeat.

I can picture it even now—
a tiny flat in London,
the kitchen painted sage green.
A simple proposal,
with my great-grandma Darlene's ring.
Our wedding photo on the mantel,
and your shoes by the door.
Our children playing in the garden
with the dog (or two or three).
Cold coffee and wrinkled bed sheets,
just us, happy as can be.

It hurts to think about
what could have been,
to grieve this future I lost.

But if you had gotten down on one knee,
I wouldn't have become this version of me.

- daydreams

I always wanted to be *that girl.*

The one who took her coffee black
and cut her own bangs
whose arms were kissed by tattoos
and her overalls splattered in paint.

The one who spent her Saturdays
at the Farmers' Market and the local coffee shop,
who always had fresh flowers and a sketchbook
and loved living life slow.

Whose room looked like something from Pinterest,
her walls covered in polaroids
of road trips with friends
and vinyl records of indie bands,
her shelves crammed with plants and books
and little knickknacks that she thrifted.

Until I woke up one day and looked in the mirror—
without realizing it, I was becoming *that girl.*
I was becoming someone
my younger self would be proud of.

I was becoming someone *I* wanted to be.

    - *unapologetically me*

Growing up, I hated the color pink.

I thought that *girly* was
synonymous with fragility,
and that loving things that were pretty
meant I lacked strength.

So I spent my *girlhood* running wild
with a bare face and scraped knees,
suppressing the softness
that lived inside of me.

I avoided lip gloss and glitter
and anything that shimmered,
because to be a *woman* is to be
condemned by anything *feminine*.

And I still don't like the color pink,
but I am learning that
embracing my *femininity*
does not make me weak.

 - femininity

You are so much like your mother.

I know they meant it
as a compliment,
but I would swear that
I was *nothing* like her.

However, her blue eyes look
back at me in the mirror—
it's like I can never escape
her judgmental stare.

But as I aged, I realized that
my teenaged rage was misplaced.
She is only human and
she did the best she could.

She is not the villain of my story,
and I am proud to be her daughter.

   - like mother, like daughter

Perhaps it's a bit cliché
for an art major to say
that Van Gogh's *Starry Night*
is their favorite work of art.

But I have always been
drawn to the stars,
and I find comfort in the
different hues of yellow and blue.

Though we are separated
by a century's worth of history,
I feel a sort of kinship
with Vincent and his story.

I put my pain into prose
while he put his into brush strokes,
but depression is not something
to be romanticized.

I must remind myself that
he was a man before
he was a painter.

He was not his illness,
and neither am I.

      - vincent

Spoiler alert: my world kept spinning,
and the sun rose again the next day.

He is neither my sun nor my stars,
and my galaxy does not revolve around him—
There is a whole damn universe out there,
so he is not worthy of any more of my tears.

  - spoiler alert

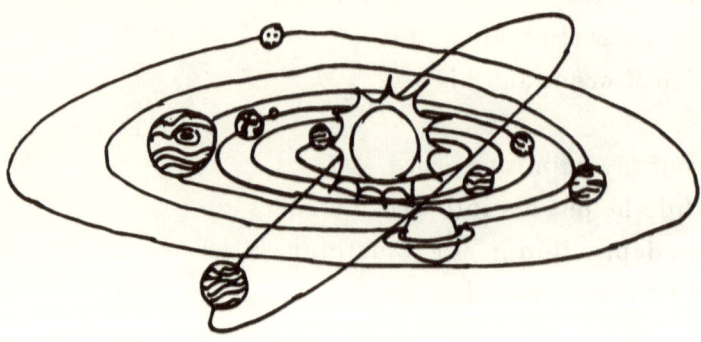

My twenties have been a *trainwreck.*

I boarded knowing my destination.
I knew where I wanted to go,
and who I wanted to be.
It was a one-way ticket
with a perfectly planned itinerary.

And it was supposed to be
a straight-forward journey,
but somewhere along the way
the *whole damn thing derailed.*

It took awhile to see,
but the carnage that
was my early twenties
shaped me.

    - *trainwreck*

He was the sun
on my rainiest days—
his rays of light chased
all of my clouds away.

Now he is gone,
yet the pain still remains.
But I am getting better
with *each passing day.*

I am learning how
to dance in the rain,
to search for rainbows
amidst all the *mundane.*

   - *storm clouds*

I am the type of girl
who wears her heart on her sleeve,
who falls in love easily,
who falls in love often:

a crowded airport
a busy bar
a bookshop aisle
a cafe window

I say that I don't believe
in love at first sight,
yet with just *one glimpse*
I see a *lifetime* in a stranger's eyes.

But I am still trying to find
empathy in mine.

- *heart on my sleeve*

Nobody notices if you skip meals
when you are already overweight
and possess a larger frame,
instead they praise your decay.

Because *skinny means pretty*,
and that's all I ever wanted to be.

It took years of counting calories
and starving my body for me to see
that being *pretty* was the
least interesting part of me.

    - recovery

Sometime between then and now,
I moved to a different state and got my own place,
where I upgraded my childhood twin to a queen bed
and my sky-blue comforter into a dark gray duvet.

I began taking my coffee black,
and ordering the occasional honey latte.
I started collecting tattoos and second-hand vinyls,
wearing Blundstones and hand-me-down overalls.

My favorite color went
from blue to gray to green.
I started spending my Saturdays
at the Farmers' Market.
I began drinking raspberry tea
and writing poetry,
I traded my moscato for Riesling,
and then mostly sobriety.

Sometime between then and now,
I found who I wanted to be.

- *transformations*

I used to believe in *destiny*,
that it was always
supposed to be
you and me.

We were tied together,
our futures intertwined
by *Fate's divine string*—
and for the longest time,
that was my lifeline.

But I was wrong and for
four years you pulled me along,
with empty promises of
becoming your wife.

I didn't see it then,
but at some point
my lifeline had *tightened
into a noose.*

And *I saved my own life*,
when I cut myself loose.

- *heart strings*

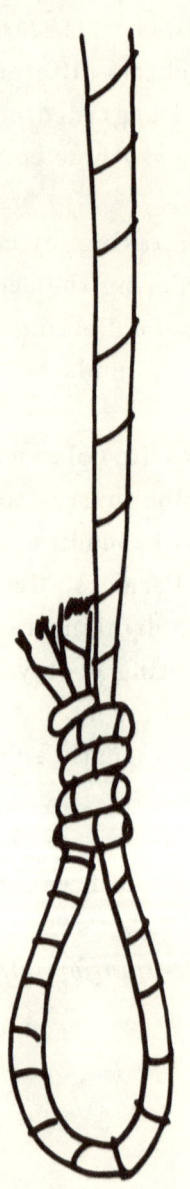

I keep playing it back,
wondering where it all went wrong,
questioning if we gave up too soon,
or if I stayed with you for too long.

But I think it was over for me
when I realized that
I loved someone else
more than I loved myself.

And if I said otherwise,
it was a *blatant lie.*

   - *lying to myself*

Growing up with brothers
is carrying scars from
overly competitive egg hunts
and backyard soccer matches.

It is spending your summer days
reading at their baseball games
and playing kick the can
and sardines in the fading light.

It is treehouse light saber fights
and near drownings during
'friendly' pool games
of sharks and minnows.

It is neighboring lockers
and shared first phones and cars,
crushing on their friends
who only know you as so-and-so's sister.

It is graduating high school
with .001 difference in GPA
and finally going your separate ways
when you attend college in different states.

It is pinching each other
during family photos,
slapping sunburns,
and poking bruises.

It is showing love
through making fun.
It is playing rough,
and growing up tough.

growing up w/ brothers

Growing up with brothers
is full of fighting and bickering
and even sometimes
just plain *hating* them.

Growing up with brothers
is watching them grow up
and become some of
your *closest friends.*

It is getting older
and moving a thousand miles away,

only to miss them *every single day.*

- *growing up with brothers*

I read somewhere that every seven years
your skin cells *regenerate*.
They get replaced one by one
until they're all *brand new*.

I don't know if that fact is true,
but instead of the heartache
I expected to feel,
all I felt was *relief*.

One day, I will have skin that
has *never* known your touch
and lips that have *not once*
tasted your kiss.

It has already been 1,308 days,
so only 1,317 more to go

u*ntil I am finally clean*.

    - *clean*

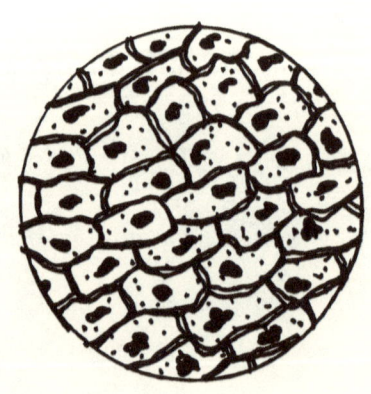

KALLIOPE KAY

He buried my memory
six feet under
and moved on
within *two weeks.*

Four years forgotten,
a warm corpse
in a fresh grave,
the flowers barely wilted.

It has been *two years*
since he broke me
and I have yet
to touch another man.

I guess that's the difference
between me and him—
I chose to break,
and he chose her.

But someday I will find someone
who makes me happy,

even if it is only myself.

    - fresh grave

He loved me then left me,
and I do not know
whether he *mourned* me
or *regrets* me—

but it truly doesn't matter,
because in the end
we are no longer together,
and our love is *dead.*

I am far better off
living only as a *memory*
stuck in his head.

- *memories*

I keep every single handwritten note and card.
I hoard ticket stubs and polaroid pictures,
piled atop crumbled *love letters*
stained with my *tears.*

All of these little mementos are
locked away in a wooden box
just collecting dust on my shelf,
but I can't find it in myself to toss.

I know that they're just things,
that mean nothing to anyone else,
but to me they are materialistic evidence
that I have *loved and lost.*

And that I'll continue to *live on*
to add more to my box.

    - *mementos*

It's only been three years
since I graduated college,
but those days seem
like a lifetime away.

Post-grad has been
moving states and
getting my own place,
figuring out life insurance and 401(k)s.

It's been most of us staying in touch
only through social media posts,
watching people we used to know
get engaged and have babies.

We're growing up,
even if it means
growing apart—
and *that's okay*.

We're on different paths,
each finding *our own way*,
but I so desperately hope that
we run into each other again someday,

even if it's only on memory lane.

    - *memory lane*

KALLIOPE KAY

I used to love the color *blue*,
and as I aged the shades matured
from *mint* to *turquoise* to *teal*
until *sky* became my favorite hue.

Then life got heavy and my hard days
became years of hidden tears,
and I was all about the color *gray*,
taupe, slate, charcoal, graphite, ash...

I said that it went with everything,
but I think maybe that shift in color
reflected the storm raging inside of me,
and sometimes, the lack of anything.

A few more years passed,
and I began to let go of my rage
and allow myself some empathy
as I started to fall in love
with the color *sage*.

Now my *grays* are slowly
being transformed into *greens*

and I think that is quite a beautiful thing.

     - color theory

Being in your twenties is scary.
You watch as your friends get engaged
and start having babies,
while you are just *burnt out and lonely.*

You *constantly* question if
you're saving enough money,
if you're on the right track,
and if you'll ever find somebody.

Some days you cannot find
the strength to even leave your bed.
Others, you find yourself replacing
your avocado toast for *just coffee* instead.

But you are not the same person
that you were yesterday –
You are learning from your mistakes
and *you are doing your best,*

and today, *that is enough.*

    - enough

Over the years,
I have *confided* in my journal
and it has patiently listened
with neither judgment nor interruption.

It has given me its full attention
in every single *conversation*
we never got to have.

It has lent an ear
as I *ranted and rambled*,
disclosing my insecurities and fears.

It has safeguarded my *secrets*
between its pages that
are blotted with tears
and wrinkled with wear.

So I will continue to *write*
about the things
that I cannot find
the words to speak

nor the strength to utter.

    - journaling

When someone asks me where I'm from
I never know how to respond,
because I grew up in three different states–
but in my mind, *home* was always

East Clairemont Place.

It was there that I was raised
on soccer and scooby doo,
on Sunday afternoon chinese takeaway
and overly-competitive family board games.

A decade later, I drove down my old street.

They had painted the house a different color,
but the treehouse was still there–
and just like me, the swinging bridge was
a little *worse for wear.*

At first it made me sad to see
my childhood home in disrepair,
but then I remember all of
those good years spent living there.

Although they have begun
to fade as I've aged
and some have been tainted
with misplaced rage,

I will always have my memories.

I have to remind myself that
most of my childhood was *happy.*
I grew up under a roof
with two parents who loved me,

and *I spent my girlhood laughing.*

  - east clairemont place

I was feeling gloomy and gray,
grumbling about the rainy day
as I watched the raindrops
roll down my windowpane.

I was wishing the storm clouds away,
when out of the corner of my eye I spied
a little girl with ladybug boots on her feet,
walking with her mother down the street.

The little girl's hood had fallen down
but she kept giggling and spinning around,
splashing her mother every time
she jumped in a mud puddle.

And *neither of them cared.*

They were both so happy and carefree.

That's when it hit me:
rainy days don't have to be gray.
and just because you grew up doesn't mean
that you have to stop dancing in the rain.

- *ladybug rain boots*

KALLIOPE KAY

There were years that
I didn't think I'd make it to twenty-five.
So I never let myself imagine
the woman *I could become* later in life.

I still don't know what
my future will look like,
but I am now starting to
form a picture in my mind

of gray streaked hair
and wrinkled cheeks,
with laughter lines
framing her blue eyes.

I really hope that she still paints.
That she takes her coffee black,
but enjoys an occasional honey latte.
That she lives in a home full
of plants and books and dog hair,
or whatever else makes her heart content.

and most of all, *I hope she's happy.*

    - hope

I still wonder what parts of me
you took with you when you left.

What memories remain
ingrained in your brain,
long after my scent finally faded
from your hoodies I used to steal.

All these years later,
does October remind you of my birthday?
And can you buy your girlfriend sunflowers
without me crossing your mind?

Do you still remember
my coffee order and my ring size?
Or that my favorite color
used to be sky blue?

It doesn't really matter,
because I take my coffee black now,
and losing you was the beginning
of choosing myself.

    - choosing me

I am not the same girl I used to be.

I have changed and grown
into a person that sometimes
I don't even recognize
and that scares me.

But for the first time
in recent memory,
she is living and evolving–
not just surviving,

and she is excited for
what tomorrow brings.

    - living

The girl I was at *nineteen*
would not recognize me at *twenty-three*,
and she would have found
that absolutely devastating.

But she did not know
who I could become without you
because now I'm almost *twenty-five*
and I am doing just fine.

I dyed my hair and cut my bangs.
I thrifted new clothes and got a few tattoos.
I started drinking raspberry tea
and switched to mostly sobriety.

I found new hobbies
and ways to move my body.
I learned that doing things alone
doesn't have to be lonely,

and most importantly
I discovered that

I love who I am becoming.

    - *the becoming*

The Blossoming

(Noun)

[ˈbläsəmiNG]

promising or healthy development.

When I die, inscribe my headstone with only
"Here lies the girl with sunflowers for eyes."

Bury me before the first frost
in a barren field with
a handful of *wildflower seeds*
to keep my body company,

so that when winter becomes spring
and the ground begins to thaw,
flowers will sprout from
what is left of my bones.

So that long after my memory fades
and my flesh decomposes,
my grave will *become a meadow*
where birds sing and children play.

So that in death, something beautiful
may *finally grow* from all of my pain and sorrow.

So that in death, I might finally *blossom.*

    - living will

Like we all do,
I started out *whole and new*,
untouched by the cruel hands of fate
and devastating heartbreak.

But *hard times* shaped me,
bad seasons eroded away my layers
and Kronos beat me down
until I was *weathered and worn*.

Reduced to ruins,
I decided to take the chisel
into my own hands—
I chipped away at all that remained,
carving away the hurt,
shaping the suffering,
piece by painstaking piece.

I'm still a work in progress,

but one day I'll sculpt myself
into a *masterpiece.*

  - masterpiece

He might be *just a dog* to you,
but to me, that dog is *everything*.

He was the constant in my passenger seat
for every single milestone I met:
a move across the country from
my parent's place to my first apartment,
to a rental house that's falling apart
with a yard much smaller than he deserved.

He watched me advance my career
from the fast-food service industry
to a college graduate with her degree,
from working three part-time jobs
just to make ends meet
to finally getting my big break.

He faithfully stayed by my side
through my darkest nights,
and gave me a reason to crawl
out of my bed in the morning light.

That dog licked all of my tears away.
That dog got me through my worst heartbreak.
That dog got me through my hardest days.
That dog got me through my early twenties.

That dog saved me.

- a girl's best friend

It makes my heart ache to think
that I'll never see your face again
outside the depths of my camera roll
and your grandmother's Facebook feed.

But then I remember
I picked myself up.
I put myself back together.
I created a version of me
that *I* could be proud of.

A new town that you have never visited,
a new apartment that you have never been,
a new bed that I share only with my dog,
a new set of sheets that your skin will never touch,
a new favorite drink you will never taste on my lips,
new bangs, new perfume, new piercings, new tattoos,
and a new necklace to replace the one you gave me.

I take comfort in knowing that
you will never know this new version of *me*.

She is all mine.

         - mine

KALLIOPE KAY

1. I sleep on the right side of the bed now

2. I cut my own bangs and dye my hair

3. I have an absurd amount of houseplants

4. I have a few tattoos, and plan to get more

5. I collect records and thrift little knick knacks

6. I go to the Farmers' Market
and buy myself flowers

7. I do yoga and barre,
and am beginning to read more

8. I still like sky blue, but sage green might be my
new favorite hue

9. I take my coffee black
and I love to drink raspberry tea

10. I write poems, and sometimes they're about you
—*but they're all for me.*

  - *10 facts you'll never get to know about me*

Leaving you shattered me completely,
yet you moved on within *a few weeks,*
while I endured *months*
of crying myself to sleep.

But it has been *two years*
since I let you go,
and now that Saturday in May
feels like a *million lifetime*s ago.

Because since quitting you
I have fallen in love a *thousand times*
as I tried new things and made new ties,
all whilst I rebuilt my life.

And I think the greatest lesson
you inadvertently taught me
was that *it is possible to move on*
without ever finding somebody else,

I just had to find myself.

    - rebuilding

One day you will find someone
who draws *constellations*
between your freckles
and sees their *universe*
in the depths of your eyes,

and you will laugh at the fact
that one boy ever made you cry.

But until then *you'll be just fine.*

   *- bricini**

**The Irish call freckles "bricini"*
which means "little stars"

.

Someday I will find someone
who is worth
every single one
of my lonely nights
and hard years,

someone who justifies
all of the heartbreak
and each of my tears.

But *someday* could be
a lifetime away,
so in the meantime,
I will find that person in *me*.

– *someday*

I am starting to see that I do not
owe the world constant apologies.
I am allowed to take up space,
to exist authentically.

I do not need permission
to be anything other than *me*.

    - permission

When you are young
they tell you to go off
and *build bridges*,

but all I knew how
to build were walls.

I was scared about what
people would think about me.
I was terrified that I would
disappoint my family.

So I bit my tongue until it bled,
disguising each weakness by
hiding my secrets behind a smile,
always terrified to speak my mind.

But now I see that
if I have to *burn bridges*,
those were not the paths
meant for me.

   - burning bridges

My scars are the *stories* that shaped me,
and most of mine you cannot see

because my demons
have plagued my sleep
with *nightmares* that
do not end when I wake.

But I clawed my way back
from the depths of hell,

so I will wear my scars as a *crown*
and rule my darkness
with a fury that scares
even the devil himself.

    - *scars*

In another life we bought that little London flat.

In that life we dance around the kitchen
that we painted sage green,
refrigerator light reflecting off
my great-grandma Darlene's ring.

But in this one I am still renting
in a small town across the sea.
I fall asleep all alone in my bed,
loneliness seeping into my dreams.

In this one I spend my Saturdays
at the Farmers' Market
where I buy myself flowers,
black coffee, and a croissant.

In this one I dyed my hair
and cut my bangs with kitchen shears.
I collect vinyls and tattoos
and pen poems, some about you.

In this one, I will be loved well
or *just do it myself.*

      - another life

I went on a date last night
with *somebody new*,
and it just didn't feel right,

but it wasn't because
he was *not you*.

    - moving on

I counted down the days
until I could finally escape
the confines of my family
and get *my own place.*

Now I'm *1,284 miles away*
Sitting in my first apartment,
surrounded by cardboard boxes
with my mattress on the floor.

But it's *too damn quiet.*

And no amount of Marketplace finds
will hide the truth that
home is so much more than
just four walls and a roof.

Home is waking up to the smell
of my dad's pancakes
and rolling my eyes at all of his bad jokes.
It is the sound of my little brother
talking to his girlfriend on the phone
and my twin playing Xbox in the next room,
and it is binge-watching Grey's Anatomy
and drinking strawberry daiquiris
with my mom on the couch.

It is loud and chaotic,
and overly competitive,
and sometimes messy,

but *home is family.*

   - homesick

I hate the *color yellow*,

yet *sunflowers* are my favorite flower.
I inherited that from my mother.

When I was a little girl, she taught me
to grow where I was planted
and to stand tall and proud
amongst the other flowers.

When I got older, she told me
to always face the *sun*,
even when storm clouds
block its light from my sight.

When I turned twenty-three,
we got matching *sunflower* tattoos
etched upon our ankles so that
she will forever walk beside me,

even when I live a thousand miles away.

It is a permanent reminder that
we share more than just some DNA,
blue eyes, freckles, and fair skin,
as well as a *streak of stubbornness*—

because she is my mother,
and sometimes blood runs thicker than water,
and it takes more than a few disagreements
to break that bond of unconditional love

shared between a *mother*
and *her daughter.*

    - *the lessons from a sunflower*

I know that there isn't a thing I could say
to make the thoughts in your head go away,
but I hope you know that at the end of the day,
it's all going to be *okay*.

> *- a message from my future self*

I have been at *war*
with my body
for so long that
I cannot remember
what *peace* feels like.

This is a *battle* that
I'm not sure will ever end—
this is a *fight* that
I'm not sure I can win.

But I am done being my own worst enemy.
So I will wave my *white flag*
and *surrender* my need
for a "better" body.

Instead, I will choose recovery.
I will choose to love me.

    - *civil war*

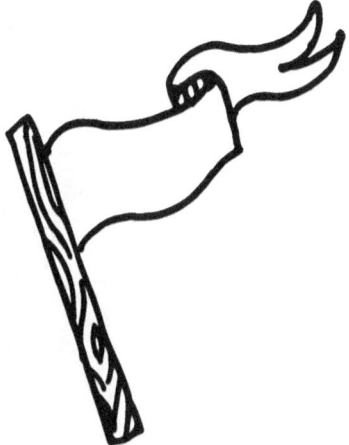

sunshine • strawberry wine • honey lattes •
summertime drives with the windows down •
hammocking with a view • sunflower fields • farmers
market bouquets • fresh chocolate croissants
• climbing the fire tower to watch the sunset
• stargazing by the dam • black coffee in your
favorite mug • avocado toast • campfire stories and
s'mores • cuddling with your dog after a long day •
curling up with a good book • bringing home a new
plant • discovering that perfect thrift store find •
lavender earl grey before bedtime • concerts at the
amphitheater downtown • rewatching your comfort
show • finally finishing that painting • kayaking
on the lake • roadtrips with your closest friends
• quiktrip slushies at exit 208 • crisp autumn air
and pumpkin spice • hiking when the leaves start to
change • fresh apple cider donuts • pumpkin patches
and hayrides • carving jack-o-lanterns • chicken pad
thai • a text from an old friend • taylor swift on the
record player • fresh tattoos • handwritten letters
in the mail • wednesday wines and spines • sushi
night • crocheting • watching christmas vacation
with your family • leaving your christmas lights up
until january • game nights • hot cocoa and fresh
snow • buying the plane ticket • visiting a new place

• dinner parties • bookstore visits • happy hour
on the patio • porch swing conversations under
twinkling string lights • pay day • strawberry
daquiris and grey's anatomy • reese's peanut butter
cups • a good sweat • yoga class • rock climbing
• sunday afternoon naps • the sound of the ocean
waves • rereading your favorite book • hot bubble
baths • weighted blankets • raspberry iced tea •
face masks and matching pajama sets • clean sheets
• hours long phone calls with long distance friends
• crab rangoon • craft nights • writing at the coffee
shop • the sound of rain on the roof • filling your
sketchbook • picnics at the park • book store visits

- serotonin

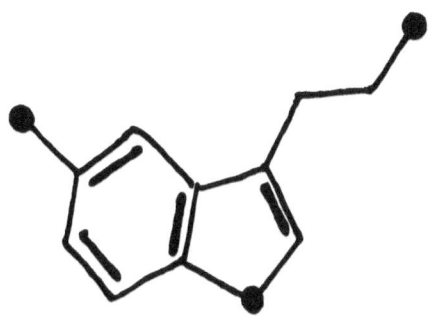

My family keeps telling me
that it's *just a phase*,
and I am going to regret
the ink on my skin someday.

But when I am wrinkled and gray,
I will look at my *tattoos* fondly
as reminders of the days when
I plastered my body with art.

The ink will fade as I age,
but will forever remain
as little time capsules
etched into my skin.

They will be small souvenirs
of the things I loved
and the stories I lived,
and *I will wear them proudly*.

Because they will remind me that
I lived for no one else but *myself*.

    - *tattoos*

When I was a little girl I wanted to be the princess
of a storybook kingdom in a land far far away
where I would find my Prince Charming
and live happily ever after someday.

but then I grew up,
and adulthood meant
being trapped in a tower
of my *own* making.

My knight in shining armor
turned out to be a dragon
who burned me with his fire,
leaving me *scarred and lonely*.

And even though there are
plenty of frogs to kiss,
none of them will
turn into my prince.

but I am *no* damsel in distress
and I will *not* spend my twenties
constantly waiting
for someone to save me.

I alone am in charge of my destiny,
so *I* will make my *own* happy ending.

    - fairytale ending

Talking about what hurt me
does not make me dramatic
or attention-seeking.
It makes me *human*.

- *notes from therapy*

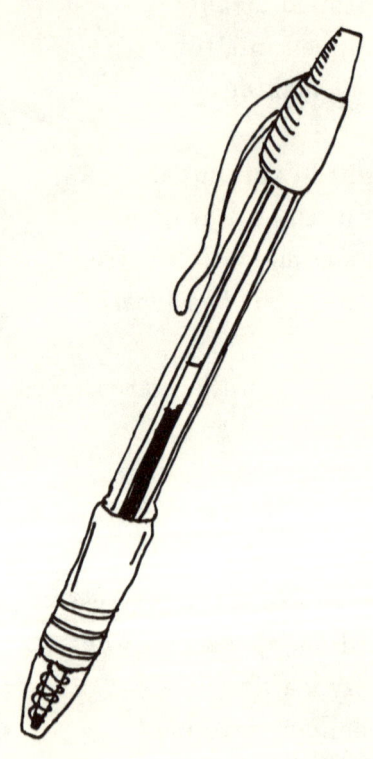

To my person,

Sixteen seems like
a *lifetime* away,
and simultaneously like
it was only *yesterday,*

But a *decade* later,

you are still the sun to my moon,
the gold to my silver,
the sugar to my cream,
and you make me a better me.

Now we live in different cities
and we're both so busy,
but somehow we didn't let
the miles tear us apart.

You are forever my person

*and you will always
have a place in my heart.*

    - *my person*

To my dearest friends,

you mended a heart you did not break
with a bond forged of years
filled with laughter and tears,
and late night talks about our hopes and fears.

We do not share any DNA
nor is the blood running
through our veins the same,
but you are *my sister*,

because in the end,
friends are the family you choose

and I am so thankful that *I chose you.*

    - female friendship

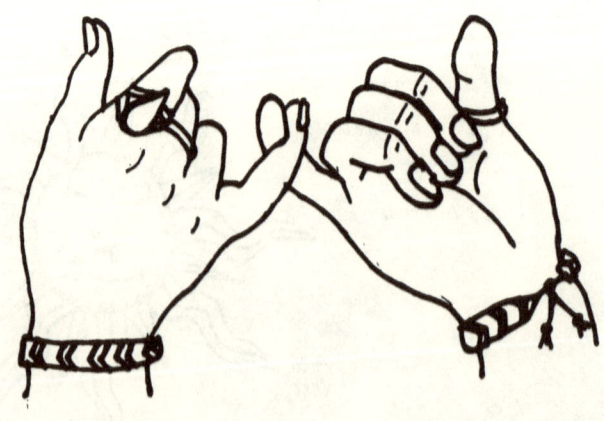

It was like you were made for me,
the way your body molded into mine
and how our lips would perfectly align—
It just felt *so right.*

Like you were my other half,
the missing piece in my puzzle,
that you completed me—
but *fuck that.*

I might be *a little* broken,
and my heart *a bit* shattered,
but I am a *whole damn* person—
all on my own.

And I do not need you.

> - *other half*

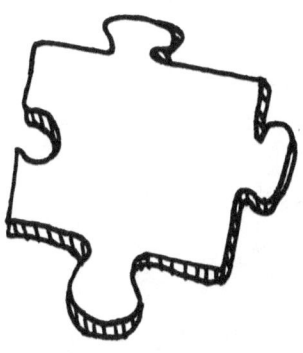

The girl I was at nineteen
thought she had it all figured out.

She had a *five-year plan*
to get that college degree
and her great-grandma Darlene's ring,
to move into that little London flat
with the kitchen painted sage green,
to adopt a dog (or two or three)
and then *eventually* have a baby.

And *it's been five years*, but somewhere along the way
the whole damn plan changed.
We tore it to shreds and sent years
of careful deliberation ablaze
with a *seven-minute* phone call
that one random morning in May.

The woman I am at twenty-four wanted more.
It may not have gone as planned,
and it certainly wasn't easy,
but we *still got the dog and the degree.*

And I am so proud
that I chose me.

      - five-year plan

KALLIOPE KAY

You loved me more at nineteen,
and I loved me more at twenty-three,

so in the end, *I chose me.*

But that doesn't mean that I didn't grieve.
I mourned the piece of me that died with us
and wept for the loss of the life we had built,
for the death of my future as your wife.

I romanticized and rationalized
and over-analyzed the past four years.
Filled with sadness, anger, and despair,
I cried until I had no more tears.

But then I dried my eyes
And slowly realized that *it gets better,*
and that I love the life I built
without you by my side,

The woman I have become at twenty-five
fills me with so much pride.

    - *better on my own*

I love you.
Three little words.
Three syllables.
One sentence.

I thought *love* was supposed to be flowers,
candlelight dinners and diamond rings,
but my friends have shown me
that *love* is a million different things.

Because what is *love* if it is not
handwritten notes on a mugs of tea
made just the way you like it—
with a splash of milk and honey.

Love is Saturday mornings
spent sitting by the pond
with a fresh croissant
and a cup of black coffee.

Love is a "text me when you make it home"
and hours spent talking on the phone.

Love is taking apart couches
and putting together bed frames
while you finish packing up
your first apartment.

Love is bringing you a container
of pasta salad because they know
you have trouble eating on the weekends.

Love is three separate conversations
on three different apps.
It is making Spotify playlists of songs
that remind you of them.

My friends have shown me that
love can be found in camaraderie.

    - love languages

You no longer get to take up
any real estate in my brain
when you are a whole world away—
so this is the *last* poem I will pen.

I know you'll probably never read this,
that these words will go unsaid.
And for that, a big part of me is glad,
but this is me finally saying goodbye.

Because I am *done* carrying hate in my heart,
so I need you to know that I wish you well,
that I genuinely hope you are happy,
and that she is everything I couldn't be.

I hope that your football club wins
(against everyone but my dad's team),
that you get to name your kid Sterling
and put him in Leicester blue onesies.

I hope you and your sister get closer,
and that you achieve all of your hopes and dreams.
I hope that you get to grow wrinkled and gray,
drinking pints with your mates at your favorite pub.

And I hope that at the end of every day,
you get to come home to the ones you love.

- this is goodbye

I am a *mosaic* of every person
I have ever loved.

I am a *puzzle* pieced together
from a thousand different
traits and habits
and little quirks,

each borrowed from a person
that I used to know.

Regardless of if
we are separated
by thousands of miles
or a lifetime of yesterdays,

they live on inside of me.

And that simultaneously
comforts and ruins me.

- *mosaic*

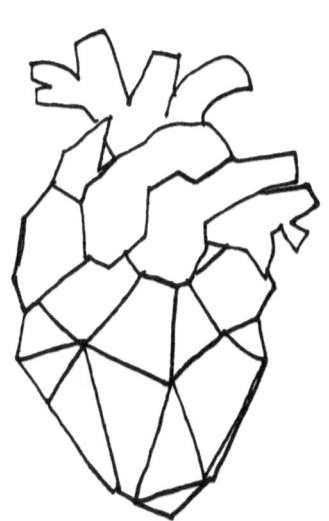

I have a callus on my middle finger—
a souvenir from my youth,
formed from years of gripping pencils
and scribbling on paper.

It's kind of ugly, but it makes me smile
because it reminds me of
that little third-grader
who had dreams of becoming a writer.

That school year,
her elementary teacher
told her to stop using
italics in her poetry

She told her that her words
needed to speak for themselves,
and that they shouldn't require
any additional *emphasis*.

It was sound advice,
but my dreams of becoming an author
came to an end not too long after that.

However, nearly *two decades* later,
I began to write again.

With each poem that I pen
I throw in a few *italics*
here and there to honor
that freckled-faced kid.

I wish she could see me
reaching for my dreams
and finally publishing
a book of poetry.

I really hope she'd be proud of me.

   - writer's bump

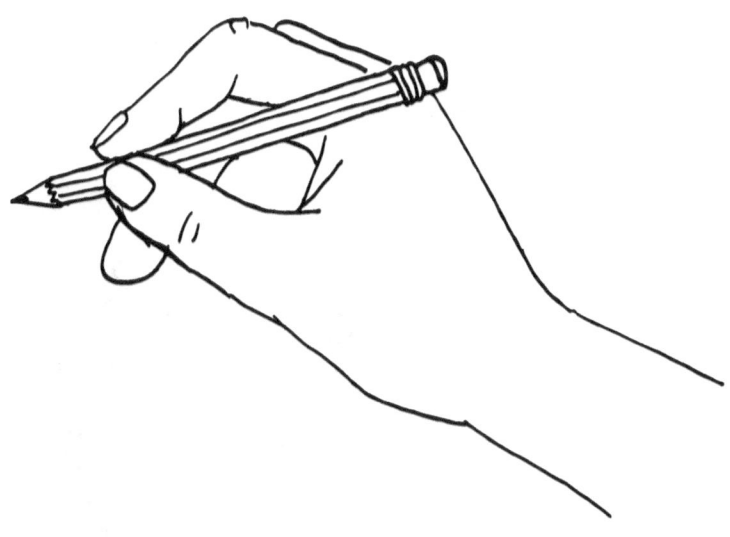

One day you're eighteen,
imagining your *someday*,
and twenty-five seems
too fucking far away,

but *almost without realizing it,*
someday fades into *today,*
today quietly becomes *yesterday,*
and then it's your twenty-fifth birthday.

Sure, it doesn't all go to plan.

Nevertheless,
you're finally living
the life younger you
only dreamed of.

You're doing the damn thing.

   - *twenty-fifth birthday*

KALLIOPE KAY

Growing up, I lived
in five different states
so home wasn't four walls and roof—
home was not a place.

For a time, I found a home in *you*,
but after four years
the foundation crumbled
and the floors rotted through.

But I will learn from my mistakes.

This time, I will build a home in *me*,
so that each time I lose my way
and after every single hard day,
I can come home to myself.

And in my new home,
I can finally rest my weary bones,
curled up by the warmth of the hearth
that I built *inside my own heart.*

   - *homebound*

You lost your way
and let yourself down.
You lied to yourself
and let yourself drown

until you hit *rock bottom*.

But you fought your demons
and now proudly carry scars
earned whilst clawing your way
out of the depths of hell.

Daughter of the moon,
just as your good days come and go,
the bad ones will come
in waves that *ebb and flow*.

You have survived everything
you have been through,
so follow the north star
that lives inside of you,

and you will survive this, too.

- the ebb and flow

This is not the end
of your story

;

a love letter for my reader

Thank you for being here.
For being tender with my poetry.

For creating a safe space
where I can bare my soul
and expose my insecurities and vulnerabilities
in complete and utter honesty.

And most of all, for continuing
to love and support me.

Yours Truly,

Kalliope

Special Acknowledgments

A special thanks to:

I. *my parents*, for never giving up on me
and loving me unconditionally

II. *my brothers*, for making me tough
and filling my girlhood with laughter

III. *the rest of my family*,
for constantly supporting my creativity

IV. *my friends*, for being the family I chose
and mending a heart you did not break

V. *my person*, for a decade of
being the sun to my moon

VI. *lyra wren*, for encouraging
and inspiring me everyday
(and letting me spam you with poetry constantly)

VII. *the team over at Outsider Poet Press*,
for taking a chance on me and making my childhood
dream of publishing a book a reality

VIII. And finally, *my readers*,
for emboldening me share my poetry

About The Author

Kalliope Kay is the writer behind ***@poetrybykalliope***. She is a twenty-something creative who lives in the Midwest with her dog. She has a Bachelors in Studio Art, and when Kalliope isn't drinking honey lattes and writing in her local bookshop's café, she spends her time freelancing, reading, painting, crocheting, traveling, and enjoying the outdoors. She loves to fill her home with art, plants, and books.

Kalliope started posting her poetry on TikTok in May of 2022. She has since expanded her social media presence across multiple platforms and grown her online following into a large community. She hopes that by sharing her story and exposing her personal struggles, she can empower others to do the same and work towards destigmatizing the discussion of mental health problems.

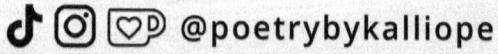 **@poetrybykalliope**

Inspired by

Alana Kirby (@alanakirbyofficial)

Alexandra Vincent (alexandra_vincent_poetry)

Ari B. Cofer (@ari.b.cofer)

bbpoetry (@bb.poetryx)

Caitlin Conlon (@cgcpoems)

Catarine Hancock (@catarinehanc0ck)

Christi Steyn (@christi.steyn.poetry)

Courtney Liadow (@courtneyliadow)

Eliana Birman (@elianabwrites)

Ellen Everett (@elleneverettpoetry)

j.lath (@j.lath_)

Law (@lawyersfather)

Lyra Wren (@poetrybylyra)

Mars (@mt.poetry)

Reva (@painonpapier)

Rose Brik (@rosebrikpoet)

Rupi Kaur (@rupikaur)

S (@allthewordsiwantedtosay)

Sabina Laura (@sabinalaura.poetry)

Sophie Diener (@sophiediener)

Whitney Hanson (@whitneyhansonpoetry)

and countless other creatives who inspire me
everyday (there's too many of you to name.)

Reference

Bare. (n.d.) In *Oxford English Dictionary*. https://
languages.oup.com/google-dictionary-en/.

Becoming. (n.d.) In *Oxford English Dictionary*. https://
languages.oup.com/google-dictionary-en/.

Blossoming. (n.d.) In *Oxford English Dictionary*. https://
languages.oup.com/google-dictionary-en/.

Break. (n.d.) In *Oxford English Dictionary*. https://
languages.oup.com/google-dictionary-en/.

Guest Contributor. (2018, June 6). *Freckles*.
Planetacom. https://www.planeta.com/
freckles/#:~:text=Ireland%3A%20
According%20to%20myth%2C%20the,in%20
English%2C%20"freckles."